FUNTASTIC!

507 Fantastic Fun Facts

Crazy Trivia Knowledge for Adults and Kids Including
Information About Animals, Space and More

ZACH OLSON

ISBN: 978-8-518596-05-4 (Paperback)
ISBN: 978-1-953991-02-7 (Hardback)

Cover design by 100Covers
Interior design by FormattedBooks

Table of Contents

Introduction

Do you want to learn new trivia and start engaging discussions with your family and friends? Or are you looking for a book that will entertain your child and help them build a love for reading? Maybe you just want a funnier life and a great read for the bathroom. It doesn't matter how old you are or what interests you generally have, this book can be enjoyed by everyone.

In *Funtastic!* you will learn 507 fantastic fun facts. These random facts about animals, science, records, money and more will entertain anyone reading them. Even if you normally are not that bookish, you can find pleasure in reading these facts. This book can help everyone start reading and establish a love for learning new things. You will laugh about the absurd facts and learn something valuable from the others. In addition, the quiz at the end is challenging and will make you curious to learn more!

About the Author

Hi, my name is Zach, and I'm a proud "hodophile." If you don't know what that means, here comes the first fact: A hodophile is someone who loves to travel. In my opinion, traveling is a must. It urges you to do things you otherwise never would. Getting out of that comfort zone is what makes your life exciting and adventurous. On the other hand, traveling also allows you to take a break, relax and appreciate your life.

Thinking about life enables new perspectives and opens one's mind. By meeting new people from various places, different world views come together. The diversity of these cultures leads to one of the most important factors of traveling: learning. It's overwhelming how many skills or amount of knowledge we can accumulate while visiting foreign countries and living unfamiliar lifestyles.

I have been traveling around the world for over a year and learned plenty of new things. Thanks to all the experiences, there's always something exciting to talk about, be it a cool story, a great joke, or an interesting fact. I always get great feedback on the facts I tell, and they often result in heavy but interesting discussions. That's why I started a list with funny and exciting knowledge that ended up becoming this book.

Hopefully, this inspires you to be more curious about life, develop a joy of discovery, and maybe even start traveling around the world.

So let's dive right into it...

PS: Do you want my next book for FREE? Then scan the QR code or click the link below :)

https://starkingbooks.activehosted.com/f/3

· 1 ·

ANIMAL KINGDOM PART 1

Let the journey begin! Millions of years before humans evolved from apes, animals had already conquered the earth. Many of them, like dinosaurs and mammoths, have died out, but others survived and developed until present day.

Nowadays, most households have a pet; in the US, the pet ownership rate is 67%. It's no coincidence the dog is called "man's best friend." This shows the popularity of animals in the modern world. And if somebody doesn't have a pet or just wants to see some more exotic animals, they can simply visit the zoo next door. Zoos achieve something extraordinary; animals that would live huge distances away from each other are now neighbors. Lions living in the desert, fishes living in the ocean, monkeys housing in the jungle, and much more – we can visit them all in just one hour of strolling around.

Although we can see many different animals, they only represent a fraction of all the species existing on this planet. It's impossible to say how many there are; some of them are living in inaccessible places and some are too small to be found. Overall, it's just insane to count every single animal on the planet. Scientists estimate that around 1 to 2 million species exist. How many of them do you know? And what do you know about them? In this chapter, you are definitely going to learn something new about these various creatures.

#1 If you keep a goldfish in the dark, it will become pale.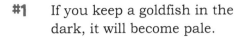

#2 Foxes have whiskers on their legs. They help them keep their bearings, especially when it's dark outside.

#3 The *Goliath Frog* is the most giant frog in the world and can grow up to 12.5 inches (32cm) in length and weigh up to 7.2 pounds (3.3kg).

#4 On a flight in the Congo, a crocodile escaped from a duffel bag, causing everybody to run to the front of the plane. Out of balance, the plane crashed, leaving only one survivor.

#5 Reindeer are able to see UV light.

#6 *Turkey Vultures* use defensive vomit. They can spit their vomit up to 10 feet (3 m).

#7 A swan, which is the largest member of the goose and duck family, has over 25,000 feathers on its body.

#8 The group of multiple whales is called a *pod*.

#9 Bumblebees have hair on their eyes.

#10 The heart of a giraffe pumps twice as hard as a cow's heart, in order to get blood to its brain.

#11 The *mongoose*, that weasel-like creature, is one of those rare animals that is immune to a snake's venom.

#12 Dogs can be allergic to humans – mainly their dander.

#13 Except for a few organs, caterpillars liquefy almost completely while undergoing metamorphosis.

#14 The *Cesky Terrier* (around 350 of them exist in total, worldwide) is the rarest breed of dog in the world.

#15 After just a few hours of being born, baby horses can walk and run.

#16 The *Saltwater Crocodile* has the highest bite force of any animal. However, the muscles to open the mouth are weak. You could shut its mouth with a couple layers of duct tape.

#17 *Pitbulls* are highly ranked among the most affectionate and least aggressive dogs. They are only aggressive when trained as such (usually for illegal dogfighting).

#18 Some butterfly species are speedy; the *Skipper Butterfly* can fly faster than a horse can run.

#19 If rabbits are approached by a predator when they are unaware, they can be literally "scared to death."

#20 *"Ear furnishings"* are those cute furry bits inside a cat's ear. They help them to hear well and ensure that dirt doesn't go inside.

#21 If a snake has its head chopped off, that clipped-off head can still bite and unleash a massive amount of venom.

#22 The only species of spider classified as vegetarian is the *Bagheera Kiplingi Spider*, which was discovered in the 1800s.

- -

#23 Kangaroos keep growing until they die. They are the world's largest marsupial.

- -

#24 Jellyfish are considered biologically immortal. They don't age and will only die if they are killed.

#25 Probably, young *Tyrannosaurus Rex* had a thin coat of downy feathers to stay warm. As they got older, they did not need them due to their size.

#26 Owls have specialized feathers. The edges protrude out to dissipate airflow, which means they can fly silently and are very deadly hunters.

#27 Waxworms can eat and break down plastic bags. This was found out by an amateur beekeeper and a group of scientists. The settings of the stomach of a waxworm can be recreated to dispose of plastic bags and bottles safely.

#28 If their mate dies, elephants can die of a broken heart.

#29 The cat's front paws are different from the back ones. On the front, they have five toes but only four on the back.

#30 Dolphins can be used for locating underwater mines and rescuing lost naval swimmers. Both the *US Army* and *Soviet militaries* have trained dolphins for this purpose.

#31 *Roselle* is a guide dog who led her blind owner down 78 flights of stairs during 9/11. They both safely made it out, even though the descent took about an hour.

#32 Ant queens may live for up to 30 years.

#33 The bigger the brain of an animal, the longer they will yawn. An animal's yawn is based on how large its brain is.

#34 *Bookworm* is a general name for insects that bore holes in books. Paper lice, for example, feed on microscopic mold in poorly kept books.

#35 *John Quincy Adams* kept a pet alligator in one of the White House bathtubs and enjoyed showing it off. He got it from a French general.

#36 *Dingoes*, which are about the same size as a *Springer Spaniel*, are brave enough to attack an adult kangaroo when hunting in packs.

#37 In the US, approximately 1,000,000 dogs are named as the heirs of their owners' wills.

#38 The hugest species of hamster is the "European" or "Common hamster" (*Cricetus cricetus*). It has a length of up to 34 cm (13.3 in), plus a tail length of 6 cm (2.4 in), yielding a total length of up to 40 cm (15.7 in). It can live for eight years.

#39 Gorillas are able to catch human colds and other illnesses.

#40 Researchers found that the loudness of a monkey is relative to the size of its testicles — the smaller the testicles, the louder the monkey.

#41 Zebras only have one toe on each foot.

#42 The *Bumblebee Bat* weighs about the same as a US dime. It's the world's smallest mammal. Native to Myanmar and Thailand, these bats are endangered.

#43 The national animal of Scotland is the unicorn.

#44 Studies have proven that llamas can be used as guards against coyote attacks on sheep herds. Just one llama is an effective protector and able to kill the attacking coyotes.

· 2 ·

WORLD AND NATURE

After observing the animals inhabiting this world, it's time to look at the wonderful planet we are all living on. 299 million years ago, all of the earth's landmass formed the supercontinent *Pangea*. Over the years, different landmasses broke apart. They episodically and slowly constituted the continents we now know. This separation and isolation of continents is why they all are unique: different continents, different landscapes, different climates. But also diverse countries, populations, languages and more have developed. It's incredible how the earth has evolved, but still remains the same.

"See the world like an artist" is one of my favorite sayings, be it the mountains, the ancient sights, or the extraordinary design of a leaf. We tend to forget the beauty of the earth, instead of being grateful for this artwork of nature. Also, the accomplishments of humankind are incredible. We have built breathtaking constructions in impossible places on the earth, and multiple populations established various cultures, cities, and countries.

To this date, 195 different countries exist. It's so exciting to explore all these foreign places and experience their cultures. Now, you can discover some interesting facts about this world.

#45 In China, there's a series of underground tunnels running 3,000 miles (4,800 km) long.

#46 In Australia, there are nearly twice as many kangaroos as there are humans.

#47 In a few *Appalachian forests,* some fireflies glow blue instead of flashing yellow.

#48 In Scotland you can travel over the same viaduct as the *Hogwarts Express.*

#49 The only continent turtles don't live on is Antarctica.

#50 Great Britain is connected to continental Europe by an area of land called "Doggerland." In 6500-6200 BC, it was flooded by rising sea-levels, turning Great Britain into an island.

#51 *Lake Superior* (Canada and US) contains 10% of the world's freshwater. It is as big as South Carolina and includes 2,900 cubic miles (12,090 km^3) of water.

#52 Only 45% of the London Underground is under the ground.

#53 Switzerland has one of the highest gun ownership rates in the world, but violent, gun-related street crime is extremely rare. In an average year, for every 200,000 of the population, there is only 1 gun murder (in the US: 24).

#54 In Indiana, there is a town called *Santa Claus*.

#55 Japan may be the cleanest country. For 12 years of school life, cleaning time is a part of the students' daily schedule, and Japanese people rarely leave rubbish on the streets.

#56 There is a Japanese village called *Nagoro* which has 35 inhabitants, but over 350 scarecrows!

#57 In Cambodia, people train rats to sniff out landmines. They can clear 200 square meters (2,000 square feet) in less than 35 minutes, which usually takes 2-3 days with a de-miner.

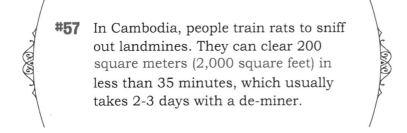

#58 The spectacular *Great Wall of China* is 21,196 km (13,170 mi) long.

#59 Sweden is the country with the most islands in the world. It has 221,800 islands.

#60 Once, Madagascar was an area for lemurs the size of today's gorillas.

#61 Over a million people live in nuclear bunkers underneath the streets of Beijing.

#62 The *Leaning Tower of Pisa* got its title because of the soft soil it's built on – This smooth soil also protected it from at least 4 powerful earthquakes.

#63 *Pig Beach* is an uninhabited island in the Bahamas which is populated entirely by swimming pigs.

#64 The German highway (called *Autobahn*) is famous for not having any speed limits. Although, in reality, around 30% of the roads do have limitations.

#65 It takes longer to drown in salt water than in freshwater. This may be the reason that around 90% of drownings occur in freshwater.

#66 Sudan has 255 pyramids. That's more than any other country. This even outnumbers Egyptian pyramids by twice the number.

#67 Probably the most widely used sign for medical assistance actually is the *Swiss flag* (white cross on red background). The reverse version (red cross on white background) would be correct, as it's the symbol of the *Red Cross*.

#68 Dinosaurs lived on every continent when they roamed the earth, including Antarctica.

#69 The *Great Pyramid of Giza* has 8 sides, rather than 4. All the other pyramids have just 4 sides.

#70 All the paint on the *Eiffel Tower* weighs as much as 10 elephants. It gets repainted every 7 years without closing to the public.

#71 Iceland does not have a railway system.

#72 The quietest room in the world is located in Minnesota. It is measured in negative decibels – so low that you can hear your heart beating.

#73 Over 65,000 pairs of *white-capped albatross* live on an island in New Zealand called "Disappointment Island."

#74 China is spending $3 billion to build panda-shaped solar farms to get more young people interested in renewable energy.

#75 Between North and South Korea lies 155 miles (250 km) of no man's land where hundreds of rare animal species thrive.

#76 *Monowi* is a town in Nebraska with a population of 1. The only resident is a woman who is the Mayor, Bartender and Librarian.

#77 The world's only country named after a woman is *Saint Lucia*.

#78 *Forrest Fenn*, who is an art dealer and author, hid a treasure chest in the Rocky Mountains worth over 1 million dollars. It still has not been discovered. (Update: *Fenn* announced the treasure was found in 2020)

#79 *Maine* is the only state in the United States that has a one-syllable name.

#80 The full name of *Los Angeles* is "El Pueblo de Nuestra Senora la Reina de los Angeles de Porciuncula".

#81 On the 18th of February 1979, it snowed in the *Sahara Desert* for 30 minutes.

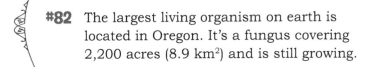

#82 The largest living organism on earth is located in Oregon. It's a fungus covering 2,200 acres (8.9 km^2) and is still growing.

#83 A tsunami caused by an underwater earthquake can travel as fast as a jet plane.

#84 Every minute there are 2,000 thunderstorms on earth.

#85 In Iceland, ice caves exist that have hot springs.

#86 In one year, over 1,200 tornadoes strike American soil.

#87 *Yuma* (Arizona) is the sunniest place on earth. It gets over 4,000 hours of sunshine a year (average 11 hours daily). The least sunny location is the *South Pole*, where the sun only shines on 182 days of the year.

#88 A flash of lightning is five times hotter than the sun.

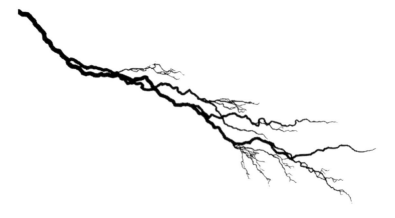

#89 Water covers 70% of the earth.

#90 Only 3% of the water on the earth is fresh, the other 97% is salted.

#91 In Australia's *Daintree Rainforest* grows a tree called the "Idiot Fruit."

#92 *Killer Whales*, also known as *Orcas*, aren't even whales. They are a type of dolphin and the hugest breed of dolphins in existence.

#93 Around 48% of the population in Uganda is under 15 years old.

- -

#94 Nearly 3% of the ice in Antarctic glaciers is penguin urine.

- -

· 3 ·

SPACE

If you think about it, this huge earth we are living on is only a tiny piece of a much bigger unit, the universe. It seems endless, and this is what makes it so fascinating. Many kids dream of becoming an astronaut, being able to float in space and making happy air jumps on the moon. But by seeing the earth from the perspective of an astronaut, we get a better understanding of how little our world is compared to the whole.

Our solar system contains 8 planets (Mercury, Venus, Earth, Mars, Jupiter, Saturn, Uranus and Neptune), without counting dwarf planets. And that's just the beginning because not only the sun (which is a star if you didn't know), but nearly all stars have planets in their own solar systems. And a large part of them are likely to have more planets than our sun. Looking to the night sky, we realize this enormous amount of stars and, therefore, the even bigger number of existing planets. We're talking about trillions of planets in our galaxy alone, and our galaxy isn't the only one in the universe. At least 200 billion other galaxies are out there!

Scientists concluded that this giant universe is filled with around 10^{25} planets. For those wondering, this number is called *ten septillion* and looks like this: 10,000,000,000,000,000,000,000,000. With continuing research, that number is going to become more accurate, but don't get lost in the numbers. What we are looking for on these planets is water and signs of life; that's where the interesting part begins.

#95 On Neptune, each day lasts for around 16 hours and 6 minutes.

#96 A booklet was written explaining how to observe Ramadan while in orbit because a Muslim astronaut had trouble fasting for Ramadan in space.

#97 Spacesuits take 5,000 hours to make, cost 1 million dollars, weigh about 110 pounds (50 kg), and have 11 layers of material.

#98 The first permanent crew inhabiting the *International Space Station (ISS)* started in 2000.

#99 The first soft drink ever consumed in space was *Coca-Cola*.

#100 The tallest mountain in our solar system, *Olympus Mons* (on planet Mars), is 3 times higher than Mount Everest.

#101 There is a *geocache* on the International Space Station. It was placed in 2008.

#102 The first game played in space was *Starcraft* – Daniel Barry took it with him in 1999, on the Space Shuttle mission STS-96.

#103 Russia has the most human-made satellites in orbit (1,324). In total, 2,271 satellites exist, and the US is in second place with 658 satellites.

#104 An 11-year-old girl suggested the name for "Pluto" after the *Roman god of the Underworld.*

#105 500 seeds of 5 different types were taken into orbit around the moon and brought back. After being planted around the US, as well as in a few other countries, they were called *Moon Trees.*

#106 Sometimes, Pluto is closer to the Sun than Neptune – one of these timelines was from 1979 to 1999.

#107 In space, humans get a little taller because there is no gravity pulling down on them.

#108 In space, the first food eaten by humans was applesauce.

#109 Even in a spaceship, birds cannot live in space because they need gravity to swallow.

#110 On the planet Venus it rains metal.

#111 The rust covering Mars' surface makes the planet appear red.

#112 The moon is very hot. During the day, the temperature can reach 260 degrees Fahrenheit (127 degrees Celsius). But when the sun goes down, temperatures can dip to minus 280°F (minus 173°C).

#113 The sun weighs about 330,000 times more than the earth.

#114 All eight planets in the *Solar System* orbit the sun in the direction of the sun's rotation. Six of them also rotate in this same direction (counter-clockwise). Venus and Uranus are the exceptions, with retrograde rotation.

#115 Even in a spacecraft, a trip to Pluto would take 9-12 years.

#116 It takes light 8 minutes and 19 seconds to travel from the sun to earth.

#117 Footprints on the moon will be there for a million years because there is no wind to erode the surface and no water to wash the prints away.

#118 More stars exist in space than grains of sand are on the world's beaches and deserts.

#119 More than 125 billion galaxies are in our universe. The galaxy we live in has about 100-400 billion stars.

#120 The formation of a *black hole* is caused by the collapse of a large dying star. It has a powerful gravitational force that sucks in everything, including light!

#121 The sun is so big, one million earths could fit inside it!

· 4 ·

FOOD AND BEVERAGES

We, our muscles and our organs, consist of the food and drinks we consume. Our bodies digest what we feed them because that's all it has. No wonder the fast-food eater isn't really that fast, but the one eating healthy foods is filled with energy and motivation to exercise and make things happen.

Our ancestors needed to hunt, collect, and pick berries to survive. Without being active, they weren't able to live. Nowadays, however, it's possible to eat in a restaurant, take your food on the go or even order it at home. This evolution of eating is why we forgot the importance of our nurture. More processed foods, unhealthy beverages and sugary cereals are now on the market and consumed in masses, daily.

Maybe you once learned *"The Food Pyramid,"* but with the forgotten significance of eating, you may have forgotten this useful scheme. If you don't know what it is, I recommend you do some research. The hierarchy represents how much you need of what nutrients; basically, it explains how to eat healthy. Here's a quick list of them, beginning at the top, with the ones you should eat the least: Food and drinks high in fat, sugar, and salt. One level lower: fats, spreads and oils. After that, meat, poultry, fish, eggs, beans and nuts. Followed by milk, yogurt and cheese. Nearly at the bottom, whole-meal cereals, breads, potatoes, pasta and rice. And finally, vegetables, salads and fruits. It needs to be added that water is always the best option to drink.

In my opinion, it's no problem to eat something sweet or some fast-food now and then, as long as it's in moderation. But remember how essential it is to stay healthy and which food and drinks do help you accomplish that.

#122 One bottle of *Coca-Cola* has a pH scale of 2.8, meaning it could dissolve a nail in just four days.

#123 When tea started being sold in bags, initially it was intended to be removed from the bags before brewing. However, customers found it easier to brew the tea still in the bag.

#124 On a genetic level, the fungus is more closely related to animals than to plants.

#125 Cucumber can cure bad breath. If you press a slice to the roof of your mouth for 30 seconds, it allows the phytochemicals to kill the problematic bacteria.

#126 Worldwide, *Subway* has more chains than the fast-food juggernaut *McDonald's*.

#127 Eating a banana can help to prevent heartburn from getting worse.

#128 Carrots have nearly zero fat content and a water content of 86-95%.

#129 Robert Chesebrough, the inventor of *Vaseline*, ate a spoonful of the stuff every single day.

#130 Drink green tea before going to bed. This will burn calories while sleeping. Green tea will also increase your metabolism.

#131 Nearly every brand of hard liquor (bourbon, vodka, whiskey, rum, gin) is vegan.

#132 The inside of a banana skin can polish leather products like handbags or shoes. Simply rub it on and wipe it off with a cloth.

#133 Although several brands claim their soda is older, *Schweppes* is widely considered the most antique one in the world. It was founded in Geneva in 1783. In addition to carbonated mineral water, *Schweppes* sells ginger ale and tonic water.

#134 Many families in Japan eat chicken from *KFC* for Christmas dinner. They order their meals months in advance and queue for hours to collect them.

#135 A natural way to deal with sunburn is by applying non-fat yogurt to a sunburnt area.

#136 Throwing an apple to a woman was considered a symbolic declaration of love in Ancient Greece. And catching it was to show acceptance of that love.

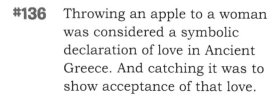

#137 Lettuce is actually a member of the sunflower family.

#138 35,000 hectares (70,000 football fields) of peas are grown in the UK in a single year.

#139 Russians think that eating ice cream will keep you warm.

#140 In Bruges (Belgium) is an underground pipeline that runs 2 miles (3.2 km) to transfer the beer from a brewery to the bottling plant.

#141 In 18th Century England, owning a pineapple was a symbol of wealth because of its high import fees.

#142 When water freezes to ice, it will take up 9% more volume.

#143 About 700 grapes go into one bottle of wine.

#144 In 2016, *Domino's* started testing pizza delivery via reindeer in Japan. It failed.

#145 *Tic Tacs* got their name from the sound made when they are tossed around in their container.

#146 Although there is currently no drug that has been proven to make someone tell the truth, some countries like India, and Russia use *truth serums*.

#147 Try chewing gum when you're writing a difficult test. It boosts mental proficiency and is considered a better test aid than caffeine.

#148 During the Second World War, a *US naval destroyer* won a battle against a *Japanese submarine* by throwing potatoes at them. The Japanese thought they were grenades.

#149 Vanilla flavoring is sometimes made with the urine of beavers.

#150 Almonds are members of the peach family.

#151 If you eat them with your nose plugged, an apple, potato, and onion all taste the same.

#152 Peanuts are one of the ingredients needed to make dynamite.

#153 Cans of diet soda will float in water, and regular soda cans will sink.

#154 Bananas are curved because they grow against gravity and towards the sun.

#155 Baby koalas are fed poop by their parents after they are born, which helps them digest eucalyptus leaves later in life.

#156 Apples float on water!

#157 Tomatoes, cucumbers and avocados are fruits, not vegetables.

·5·

SPORTS AND OTHER ACTIVITIES

"Sport ist Mord" is a German saying, meaning that sports are murder. In some way, it's true because sports can encourage injuries and long-term damage to your body. On the other hand, physical activities are fun (for most people), free the mind, and get your body working.

Sports have been a significant theme throughout human history. In the beginning, they were often used as preparation for hunting or fighting. In 776 BC, the first Olympic Games were held by the Ancient Greeks;

they included activities such as wrestling, races, jumping, and discus throwing. More than 2,000 years later, the Olympic Games are still running and astonishing millions of people all over the world. Championships like this create a stronger bond between the inhabitants of each country and connect the different nations.

But sport doesn't only mean playing soccer or working out. other activities like hiking or going to work on foot will make you a more active person. The human body needs to be challenged, otherwise it will get bored and depressed. If muscles never get used, they will start to regress. That's why it is crucial to participate in some sort of physical activity. Not only will your body know that it's needed, but also will feel awesome after finishing an intensive training.

The same way a workout can exhaust and train your body, it's possible to exercise your brain. This is equally as important, and you are doing it right now. Great job; keep going!

#158 Baseballs had initially been made from the foreskins of horses.

#159 Cricket is the second most popular sport in the world (after soccer/football).

#160 An average golf ball has around 336 dimples.

#161 The UK parliament banned females from participating in dangerous sports.

#162 Olympic gold medals are made of silver.

#163 Actual playing time in a *major league baseball* game is on average less than 18 minutes.

#164 More than 100 million people worldwide have licenses for hunting.

#165 Golf balls were originally made of cow or horsehide and stuffed with feathers, most often goose feathers.

#166 In the ancient *Greek Olympics*, all wrestling matches were in the nude.

#167 At the *2008 Beijing Games*, the Chinese won 100 medals.

#168 The *National Basketball Association (NBA)* was founded on the 6th of June in 1946.

#169 *Extreme ironing* originated in England. It is a sport in which people take ironing boards to remote locations and iron items of clothing.

#170 Alongside chess, Sudoku has been named as one of the best ways to improve the mind and memory.

#171 While walking, you're using a total of 200 muscles with every step you take.

#172 *Gatorade* was invented more than 40 years ago to help the Florida Gators Football Team stay hydrated.

#173 The longest cricket test match, which was held between England and South Africa, lasted over 12 days. It only finished because the English team would have missed their boat home.

#174 Originally, bumper cars weren't supposed to hit each other. Drivers were supposed to avoid crashing despite chaotic driving.

#175 In 1912, the last Olympic gold medals made entirely from gold were awarded.

#176 At the *1908 Olympics* in London, the Russians showed up 12 days late because they used the Julian calendar instead of the Gregorian one.

#177 There exists an underwater version of rugby, unsurprisingly referred to as "underwater rugby."

#178 Did you know that 78% of former NFL players have gone bankrupt or are under financial stress by the time they have been retired for 2 years? This is mostly because of joblessness or divorce.

#179 *Wilt Chamberlain* scored 100 points in one single NBA basketball game (1962). No one has broken this record since then, not even Steph Curry!

#180 The record for the longest jump is held by *Mike Powell*: 29 ft. + 4 inches (8.95 m). That's about like jumping the length of two minivans!

#181 *NFL Super Bowl* referees also get Super Bowl rings.

#182 Cleveland Indians' pitcher *Ray Caldwell* was struck by lightning during a game in 1919. He kept playing!

· 6 ·

SCIENCE AND NUMBERS

To understand how the world works – that's the goal of every scientist, and it has been that way for many, many years before us. Thanks to curious minds like *Thomas Edison* (who invented the light bulb), our world is much more enjoyable than it was hundreds of years ago.

The development of the earth is insane. In 1946, the first computer filled a large room and needed several people to operate. Less than 100 years later, a smartphone as small as a hand and operated by only one finger can do things the first computer couldn't even imagine. But not only technology improved, also biology, chemistry and many more thematic fields were expanded.

For instance, new treatments for the *Ebola disease* have been found. Thanks to improved science, we now know that the virus attacks the immune system and can cause organ failure, resulting in thousands of deaths. In addition to a proven vaccine, researchers have been seeking treatments for patients who already were infected. This is only one example. Countless other discoveries changed the world immensely, like the *periodic table*, the structure of *DNA*, *electromagnetism* and Einstein's *Theory of Relativity*.

The list is endless, and every day, new case studies are conducted. Nevertheless, we are far from understanding everything. That's why we must always seek more education, more knowledge, and more facts.

#183 It is shown that using a hands-free device to talk on the phone while driving is equally or more dangerous than driving drunk.

#184 Daily, 27,000 trees are cut down to supply toilet paper for the world.

#185 When you think of a past event, you remember the last time you remembered it, not the occasion itself.

#186 Giving up alcohol for just one month is very healthy. It improves liver function, decreases blood pressure, and reduces the risk of liver disease and diabetes.

#187 The consumption of sugary drinks is linked to 180,000 deaths per year.

#188 "Cars.com" was the most expensive domain name ever sold. Astonishing fact, that it cost $872.3 million.

#189 While playing offline games on your phone, putting it in airplane mode will stop the ads.

#190 Computers designed for Amish people have selling points like "*No internet, no video, no music.*" They really do exist.

#191 Butterflies have an exoskeleton, meaning their skeletons are on the outside of their bodies

#192 In general, people tend to read 10% more slowly from a screen than from paper.

#193 Seven to eight trees are needed to provide enough oxygen for just one person per year.

#194 There is an expansive collection of books under the *British library*'s archive. If a person read 5 books per day, it still would take 80,000 years to complete the whole collection.

#195 Deep snow can sometimes appear blue because the extra layers of snow create a filter for light.

#196 Most customers look at the reviews of a product before they buy it. Reviews help to build trust and can increase the popularity of a product drastically. Why don't you leave a quick review for this book when you finish it :)

#197 The most expensive substance available in the world is *antimatter*. It costs about $62.5 trillion per gram.

#198 If you multiply 1,089 by 9, you get the exact reverse, 9,801.

#199 Roughly 15% of active *Twitter* accounts are social bots. Meaning there are nearly 48 million accounts that are controlled by computers.

#200 The use of tanning beds before age 30 increases your risk of developing *melanoma (skin cancer)* by 75%. Tanning beds and lamps are in the highest cancer risk category.

#201 Babies have more bones than adults. As they grow up, some bones fuse to form one bone. Newborns have around 305 bones, adults 206.

#202 The *water dropwort* is a highly toxic plant. If it kills you, it can make you smile after you die. This smile is called a sardonic grin.

#203 *Volvo* invented the three-point seatbelt and then gave the invention away for free. They decided it was too important an innovation to keep to themselves.

#204 Rubber bands last longer when they are refrigerated because it makes the polymers more relaxed.

#205 Any prime number higher than 3, if squared and subtracted by one, will always turn out to be a *multiple of 24.* 5, 7, 11, 13... you can try it out!

#206 The *Star Wars* lightsaber's sound was created by combining the sound of an idle film projector and the hum from an old TV set.

#207 Cranes are built using cranes. But how was the first crane built?

#208 Surgeons who play video games at least 3 hours a week perform 27% faster and make 37% fewer errors during surgery.

#209 Cold showers have more health benefits than warm ones. Advantages include improvement of circulation, stimulating weight loss, and easing depression.

#210 Before Apple bought *Siri*, it was initially going to be released as an app for Android & Blackberry.

#211 Albert Einstein (1879 - 1955) had mastered *calculus* by the tender age of 15.

#212 A study from *Harvard University* found that having no friends can be just as deadly as smoking. Both of them affect levels of a blood-clotting protein.

#213 Amber-colored rear turn signals are statistically proven to reduce collisions by about 28%.

#214 In poker, the odds of getting a *royal flush* are precisely 1 in 649,740.

#215 Gaming-related accidents increased by 26.5% during the first five months of *Pokémon Go* being released. This included two deaths and $25.5 million in damages.

#216 When you shuffle a deck of cards, the number of possible arrangements is *52!* (52 x 51 x 50 x 49 x ... x 3 x 2 x 1). This number is higher than the number of stars in the observable universe.

#217 If you heat a magnet, it will lose its magnetism.

#218 Violin bows are commonly made from horsehair.

#219 Pointing your car keys to your head increases the remote's signal range.

#220 Wearing headphones for just 1 hour could increase the bacteria in your ear by 700 times.

#221 Glass balls can bounce higher than the ones made of rubber (providing they don't break).

#222 A year has 31,556,926 seconds.

#223 There is a 50% chance that in a room with 23 other people, 2 of them will share a birthday.

#224 Number *four* is the only one with the same number of letters as its value.

#225 The opposite sides of the dice always add up to seven.

#226 On average, a yawn lasts 6 seconds, and men yawn longer than women.

#227 The exposure to radioactivity not only affected *Marie Curie* (one of the most famous chemists) but also most of her belongings. Now, more than a century later, her notebooks need to be stored in a lead box, because they are still radioactive (and will be for another 1,500 years)!

·7·

HUMANS

Zoologically viewed, we humans are an upright-walking species called *Homo Sapiens* and developed from primates 315,000 years ago. Our predecessors have always shared the earth with other apelike primates, from long-extinct apes to the modern gorilla. That we are somehow related to apes is accepted by biologists and anthropologists all around the world. But since *Charles Darwin*, a great British naturalist, published his theory, the exact nature of our evolutionary relationships has been the subject of debate. Because the fossil correlation is unclear, experts can't agree on a full chronological series of species, leading to *Homo Sapiens*.

What they can agree on is that as we humans evolved, we started to populate and successfully took over the world. The Ancient Greeks, Romans, Barbarians and more, all created new colonies, spread over the continent, and expanded their empires. It took a long time of exploring, fighting and establishing, until the countries as we now know them were formed.

Nowadays, we don't have to build castles to protect our borders. And it's much easier to focus on our occupations, families and friends. Although our body has transformed through time, the human being has always been a social creature. Only because of the ability to work together, humankind was able to create such an amazing world. Humanity is just incredible!

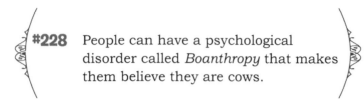

#228 People can have a psychological disorder called *Boanthropy* that makes them believe they are cows.

#229 On average, a person in New Zealand sleeps nearly 7h 45 min per day, making it the "sleepiest country" in the developed world. In Japan, people sleep around 6h 15min.

#230 Using an average of 80 beats per minute, your heart beats about 4,800 times per hour. That's a whopping 115,200 times per day.

#231 The human eye is extremely sensitive. If the earth were flat, and it was night, a candle's flame could be seen from 30 miles (48 km) away.

#232 There are 26 bones in a human foot.

- -

#233 Human beings cannot walk in a straight line without a visual point. When blindfolded, we will gradually walk in a circle.

- -

#234 Remember, next time when your throat tickles, scratching your ear can make it go away.

#235 It is possible to wake up during surgery – how terrifying!

#236 When you see someone you like, the "butterflies" you get in your stomach is a stress response called adrenaline.

#237 The distance from your wrist to your elbow corresponds to the length of your foot.

#238 Ten percent of Filipinos (approximately 10 million people) live outside the Philippines. The country with the highest number of *Overseas Filipinos* is the United States, with 4 million Filipinos.

#239 It takes a red blood cell only about 1 minute to make a complete circuit through your body.

#240 Your immune system can weaken when you are in a negative relationship.

#241 Your brain uses 20% of all
oxygen in your body.

#242 The only innate fears we have when born
are the fear of falling and the fear of loud
sounds. All other fears are learned.

#243 The tongue is the only muscle in our
body that is only attached at one end.

#244 The human eye moves about
50 times every second.

#245 About 25% of all blood coming from
the heart goes into the kidneys.

#246 Without saliva, humans aren't
able to taste food.

#247 Approximately 1 in 2,000 babies
already has a tooth when it is born.

#248 Researchers found that flossing your teeth
can help your memory. Flossing prevents
gum disease. Gum disease prevents stiff
blood vessels, which cause memory issues.

#249 Most people can't lick their elbow. (You can try it!)

#250 If you sneeze too hard, you could fracture your rib.

#251 Like fingerprints, everyone's tongue print is different.

#252 You fart an average of 14 times a day, and each fart travels from your body at 7 mph (11 km/h).

#253 The average person spends 2 weeks of their life waiting at traffic lights.

#254 Before 1913, parents could mail their kids to Grandma's – through the postal service.

#255 A typical cough is 60 mph (96 km/h), a sneeze is often faster than 100 mph (160 km/h).

#256 Sneezing with your eyes open is impossible.

#257 Some people are terrified that a duck is watching them. This is called "Anatidaephobia."

(Update: This word is not officially recognized)

#258   When you look up at a bright sky and
see white dots, you are looking at your
blood. Those are white blood cells.

#259   The teeth of humans are as
strong as shark teeth.

#260 Your nose and ears never stop growing.

#261   About 70% of an adult's body is water.

· 8 ·

LAWS AND RULES

Have you ever seen the film *The Purge*? In this film, one day per year, no rules apply, and nothing is illegal. It is always the most dangerous day of the year, which shows us how important our regulations and laws are. If we want to live in a safe, ordered country, it's crucial to have some guidelines for everyone to follow.

Back when empires had kings, it was their duty to create such rules and punish the ones who didn't obey. The same principles apply today, although, these days the power is distributed among various people, like police officers, judges, and lawyers. All of them act in favor of the security of our nation. In democracies, everyone can vote and come up with new ideas for improvements of the government. There are very few absolute monarchies, where you need to be born into a royal family in order to become the leader.

In the end, I believe the goal of every single person is to live an enjoyable life. And the law is what creates the opportunity for this livable environment. Not only are political rules essential, but at a job or in a sport, the terms also need to be set. Setting such agreements enables us to create fair conditions for each part of a deal. Laws and rules may vary from country to country, and some of them are more useful than others (you will see that in this chapter). But all in all, we need guidelines for living a pleasant lifestyle.

#262 *Kraft Singles* (and other sliced cheese) cannot be advertised as cheese. This is because *US FDA* standards state that food can only be identified as a cheese if it contains "at least 51% real cheese".

#263 It is a federal crime to use the *Netflix* account of your roommate or friend.

#264 In the Northern Territory, Australia, it is illegal to play a musical instrument on a bus.

#265 Northern Korean people are only allowed to have one of 30 haircuts. Men and women must each choose from 15 different styles , each.

#266 According to the *Texas Parks and Wildlife Department*, in Texas it is legal to kill Bigfoot if you find it because it would be considered a non-protected non-game animal.

#267 In New Jersey, it is illegal to wear a bulletproof vest while committing a violent crime.

#268 In India, a law from 1934 classes kites as an aircraft, which is why the flying of a kite is illegal.

#269 In the state of Utah, birds have the right-of-way on a freeway.

#270 In Greece, women are legally not allowed to wear high heels or tall hats in the Olympic Stadium.

#271 China banned the movie "Back to the Future" because it contained time travel.

#272 Even though smoking is prohibited on airplanes, ashtrays are mandatory on every plane. This is meant for safe disposal, in case someone breaks the law.

#273 At *Halden prison* in Norway, guards are encouraged to interact, play sports, and eat with the inmates. This is to help prevent aggression and create a sense of family.

#274 In New Delhi, if a tree gets sick, an ambulance is sent to treat it. This rule came into effect in 2009, and it takes 4 people to do the job.

#275 California law does not prohibit lane splitting. It's the only state in the US that allows motorcycles to pass other vehicles within the same lane.

#276 There are *alien abduction insurance policies*. Around 50,000 of these have been sold, mainly to residents of the US and England.

#277 All new FBI special agents and intelligence analysts have to visit the *United States Holocaust Memorial Museum*.

#278 As specified by the *US Department of Agriculture*, the definition of an original sandwich is "at least 35% cooked meat and not more than 50% bread."

#279 In Los Angeles, 50% of apartments don't come with a fridge. That's legal, as fridges are considered an "amenity," and therefore, landlords are not required to provide one.

#280 There exists a company in the UK that offers "being hungover" as a valid reason for calling in sick to work. They are allocated 4 hungover days per year.

#281 In Mexico, non-violent attempts to escape prisons are not punished because "it's human nature to want freedom."

#282 It's illegal to die in *Svalbard*, a remote Norwegian island.

#283 Only official members of nationwide, recognized Native American tribes may legally possess or collect eagle feathers.

#284 In Uganda, owners of *personalized license plates* face a tax increase of over 300%.

#285 If you cut down a cactus in Arizona, you can be punished by up to 25 years in jail. It is a crime similar to felling a protected tree species.

#286 It's illegal to own just one guinea pig in Switzerland.

#287 When playing in Wimbledon, tennis players are not allowed to swear.

#288 *Facebook*, *Twitter* and *Instagram* are all banned in China.

#289 In *Sellia* (Italy), dying is illegal. Essentially, it was meant as a nice gesture, encouraging people to take care of their health. But people who do not follow regular health checks will be fined.

#290 In the streets of London, it's illegal to beat or shake a mat, carpet, or a rug.

#291 In the United Kingdom, it's an offense to carry a plank on the sidewalk.

· 9 ·

MONEY

Money doesn't make you happy. This is said everywhere and to everyone. But what about all the things money enables you to do: taking a day off, traveling, buying presents for your loved ones, going out for dinner, and being able to afford a roof over your head. The freedom to do these things definitely helps to make me happy. Of course, it's not healthy to go overboard about money and become a workaholic in order to make as much cash as you can. But it's also extremely stressful to live paycheck to paycheck and have to cut out things you would really like to do.

Overall, money is a fascinating topic. In a nutshell, it's only printed paper or some metal coins with value assigned by society. It all started with *bartering*. That is the exchange of services or resources for a mutual advantage that dates back tens of thousands of years. Then animals, like cows, camels, and sheep, became more popular and were used as a form of money. In 1,000 BC, the first form of metal coins was manufactured by China. And in 118 BC, the first form of banknotes was used—basically, one-foot-square leather pieces with colorful borders.

Nowadays, we are still using notes, except they are made from paper instead of leather. However, the usage of paper money will probably disappear slowly. In our digital age, the future money currency may be electronic. Because most transactions take place electronically now, digital cash will most likely become the currency of the future.

#292 The *US dollar* is the most commonly used currency in the world.

#293 There are 293 ways to make change for a Dollar.

#294 Some countries share a currency. For example, multiple countries in Europe use the *Euro*.

#295 The largest bill ever printed was a $100,000 gold certificate issued in 1934.

#296 *McDonald's* makes about $75 million per day.

#297 Salt was used as a form of money by early Romans — even the word "salary" is derived from *sal*, which means "salt" in Latin.

#298 The world's most expensive object ever built is the *International Space Station* (US $150 billion).

#299 The Icelanders use credit cards and debit cards more frequently than any other country in the world.

#300 One of the first Bitcoin transactions was to buy a pizza for 10,000 Bitcoins. The worth of 10,000 Bitcoins now is $887 million.

#301 On average, an American family carries a credit card debt of $8,000.

#302 *Apple* earns US $300,000 per minute.

#303 Queen Elizabeth II (born in 1926) holds the record for her image appearing on the most currencies. She is represented on money in at least 35 different countries.

#304 Nowadays, over 170 different currencies are used around the world.

#305 Two-thirds of all printed US $100 bills are held outside the US.

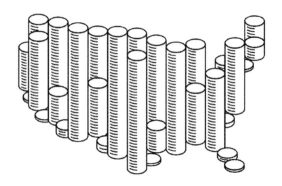

#306 In the world, more than 1.6 million ATMs exist.

#307 Pablo Picasso, who died in 1973, was the wealthiest artist in history.

#308 In 1911, *Mona Lisa* was stolen from the Louvre, which drew more visitors to see the empty space than the actual painting did.

#309 The *British Pound* is the oldest currency in the world, which is still in use (1,200 years old). Its identity is a symbol of British sovereignty.

#310 The total amount spent on adult Halloween costumes each year, in America, is $1.5 billion.

#311 During *World War II*, Germany tried to break down the British economy by dropping millions of counterfeit bills over London.

#312 Money is made in factories called mints.

#313 The first paper money was made in China over 1,000 years ago.

#314 A dime has 118 ridges around the edge.

#315 The *1913 Liberty Head Nickel* is one of the most expensive coins in the world ($4.4 million).

· 10 ·

ANIMAL KINGDOM PART 2

After reading the first chapter, you should already be an expert on this topic. However, I bet you can't remember how many different kinds of animals are living on the earth. To refresh your mind: scientists estimate that around 1 to 2 million diverse species exist. That figure has led experts to guess that the number of individual animals is *20 quintillion.* That's 20 billion billion!

Because of this great number of living animals, there is also a vast amount of facts about them. Besides, everyone loves animals, and that's why we've got a second part with surprising facts about them.

#316 Animals called *stoats* go crazy jumping, spinning, and twisting while hunting so they get a rabbit's attention. This unique technique of hunting hypnotizes the rabbit until the *stoat* gets close enough to attack.

#317 The Guinness World Record for the longest time searching for the *Loch Ness Monster* is held by Steve Feltham. He camped at Loch Ness for 25 years.

#318 If you cut a starfish, it won't bleed because it doesn't have blood!

#319 It is not only humans who are right- or left-handed. Most male cats prefer using their left paw, and females are more likely to be right-pawed.

#320 Sharks living in an active underwater volcano have been discovered by scientists. Divers are not able to investigate because they would get burns from the acidity and heat.

#321 The color *red* doesn't make bulls angry; they are color-blind.

#322 A baby panda right after birth is smaller than a mouse.

#323 The veins of a blue whale are so big a child could swim through them.

#324 Frogs drink water through their skin.

#325 A crocodile cannot stick its tongue out.

#326 Billy goats urinate on their heads to smell more attractive to females.

#327 Elephants stay pregnant for 22 months; it's the longest-lasting period of gestation in any land mammal.

#328 A shrimp has his heart in its head.

#329 Physically, it's impossible for pigs to look up into the sky.

#330 Cat urine glows under black light.

#331 The only fish that can blink with both eyes is the shark.

#332 Cats have 32 muscles in each ear.

#333 An ostrich's brain is smaller than its eye.

#334 Tigers have not only striped fur, but also striped skin.

#335 The giant squid has the biggest eyes in the world (diameter of 10 in / 25 cm).

#336 Rabbits and parrots are able to see behind themselves without even moving their heads!

#337 Butterflies taste food by standing on top of it! Unlike humans who have most taste receptors on their tongue, butterflies have them in their feet.

#338 Although the *Stegosaurus dinosaur* was over 9 meters (30 feet) long, its brain was only the size of a walnut.

#339 Kangaroos and emus struggle to walk backward because of the unusual shape of their legs.

#340 A hippopotamus may seem huge. However, it can run faster than a man. Male hippos can weigh more than 6,000 pounds (2.7 t) and females around 3,000 pounds (1.36 t). Despite their massive bulk, hippos can run up to 30 miles (48 km) per hour!

#341 Snails take the longest-lasting naps, some last as long as 3 years.

#342 Some fish cough. Really.

#343 Goats have rectangular pupils in their eyes.

#344 If a zebra and a donkey have a baby, it is called a *Zonkey*.

#345 Tiger shark embryos begin attacking each other before they are even born. The fight starts when they are still in their mother's womb.

#346 The blue whale is the largest living animal, which can measure as much as 100 feet (30 m).

#347 Nearly 10% of a cat's bones is in its tail.

#348 In the wintertime, reindeer grow their facial hair long enough to cover their mouths, which protects their muzzles when grazing in the snow.

#349 Bamboo makes up 99% of a panda's diet. Sometimes, they eat fish or small animals.

#350 Horses can sleep standing up.

#351 Slugs have four noses.

#352 Owls can't move their eyeballs because they have none.

#353 Hummingbirds, which can beat their wings up to 200 times per second, are the only birds in the world able to fly sideways, backward, up and down. They can even hover in mid-air and fly upside-down.

#354 Male ostriches can roar like lions. And generally, ostriches can run faster than horses.

#355 Usually, a lion in the wild makes no more than 20 kills a year.

#356 You can hear a blue whale's heartbeat from a distance of 2 miles (3.2 km). Its heart is the size of a small car. Naturally, this massive animal would have an equally huge heart. You might miss the heartbeat, though, since it only beats 8 to 10 times per minute.

#357 A kangaroo can't hop if you lift its tail off the ground.

#358 For two days, a swarm of 20,000 bees followed a car because their queen was stuck inside.

#359 Have you ever thought you are forgetful? Don't feel badly. Squirrels forget where they hid about half their nuts.

· 11 ·

RECORDS

Be the strongest, the smartest, the most successful. Everybody wants to be the best. It's that feeling of superiority that makes us think we are something better. But when we reach the top, most of the time, we realize that it doesn't make us happier than before. Look at "successful" people of society. For example, famous music stars often end up in drug addiction and lose everything they worked so hard for. Maybe the sudden fame is too much to handle, and they lose control.

Let's not focus on the negative, but on the extraordinary things that have been accomplished thanks to the drive to become better than everybody else. When looking at sports, some set records seem impossible for a human being; but still, a specific person was able to jump that high or throw that far. Such accomplishments should and definitely do make these athletes proud. Additionally, it can be inspiring for others to become better and work on themselves.

If you think about records, *The Guinness Book of World Records* instantly comes to mind. When looking through this book, we can read about the unbelievable records humans have accomplished. Some performances are simply overwhelming, like one person pulling an airplane or the most blindly-shot free throws in basketball. Others are less incredible and more absurd, like the loudest burp or the longest fingernails. It doesn't matter if you personally want to break that record or not, it's exciting to read about supernatural achievements, anyway!

#360 The largest human mattress domino consisted of 2,019 people (Rio de Janeiro, Brazil, on the 6th of August in 2019). The whole successful record attempt lasted 11 minutes and 13 seconds. After that, all 2,019 mattresses were donated to charities.

#361 *Chad Fell* (USA) set the record for the biggest bubblegum bubble. He blew a bubble with a diameter of 50.8 cm (20 in) without using his hands, on the 24th of April in 2004.

#362 The largest advertising poster measured 28,922.10 m² (311,314 ft²) and was produced for *Arby's* (American fast-food chain) on the 13th of June in 2018. That's four times the size of a soccer field.

#363 The most decimal places of *Pi* memorized is 70,000. It was achieved by *Rajveer Meena* (India) on the 21st of March in 2015.

#364 The widest mouth measures 17 cm (6.69 in). This gigantic mouth belongs to *Francisco Domingo Joaquim* (from Angola).

#365 The highest vehicle mileage is 3,039,122 miles (4,890,992 km). By the 1st of May in 2014, a *1966 Volvo 1800S* had driven this insane number of miles.

#366 The hugest pizza has a total surface area of 1,261.65 m² (13,580.28 ft²). On the 13th of December in 2012, it was prepared by multiple members of *NIPfood* at Fiera Roma, in Rome, Italy.

#367 *Hercules* is the largest living cat. He's an adult male *liger* (lion x tigress hybrid) and currently housed at a wildlife reserve in South Carolina, USA. He measures 3.33 m (131 in), stands 1.25 m (49 in) at the shoulder, and weighs 418.2 kg (922 lb).

#368 *Robert Pershing Wadlow* (born on the 22nd of February in 1918) is the tallest man in medical history for whom there is irrefutable evidence. When he was last measured on the 27th of June in 1940, Robert was 2.72 m (8 ft 11.1 in) tall.

#369 The longest nose of a living person belongs to *Mehmet Özyürek* (Turkey). It measures 8.8 cm (3.46 in) from the bridge to the tip.

#370 *Zeus* (USA) is the tallest dog ever. He's a *Great Dane* who was measured 1.12 m (44 in) high on the 4th of October in 2011.

#371 The longest time that breath was held voluntarily is 24 min 3.45 s. *Aleix Segura* Vendrell (Spain) accomplished this record on the 28th of February in 2016.

#372 The highest mountain in the world is *Mount Everest.* Its peak rises to 8,848 m (29,028 ft) – the highest point in the world. It takes 6-9 weeks to climb it.

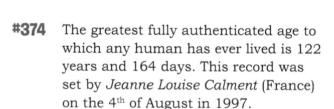

#373 The world longest fingernails belonged to *Lee Redmond* (USA). Lee started to grow them in 1979 and reached a total length of 8.65 m (28 ft 4.5 in). She lost her nails in a car accident in early 2009.

#374 The greatest fully authenticated age to which any human has ever lived is 122 years and 164 days. This record was set by *Jeanne Louise Calment* (France) on the 4th of August in 1997.

#375 *Eminem* holds the world record for the most words in a hit single. "Rap God" packs 1,560 words into a 6 min 4 sec song (on average 4.3 words per second).

#376 *Anna Bagenholm* fell through a frozen stream while she was skiing and was stuck for over an hour. Even though she was clinically dead, she made a full recovery and became the person to survive the lowest body temperature ever recorded (56.7 F / 13.7 C).

#377 In 2005, the largest pumpkin pie ever was baked. It weighed 2,020 pounds (916 kg).

#378 Belgium holds the Guinness world record for the longest time needed to create an official government (589 days).

#379 *Sonic the Hedgehog* holds a record in the Guinness Book of World Records. He is described as the fastest gaming character ever.

#380 One U.S. Park Ranger got hit by lightning seven times and survived all of them.

#381 *Garrett McNamara* holds the record for the biggest wave ever surfed, set in 2011 in Nazare, Portugal. The wave was 78 feet (23.77 m) tall. He had to get towed into the wave by a jet ski.

#382 The highest dying body count in film history goes to *"Lord of the Rings: Return of the King"* with 836 on-screen deaths.

#383 *The Guinness Book of World Records* was started by the manager of *Guinness* when he got annoyed that he couldn't find out which was the fastest game bird ever recorded.

#384 There's a world record for the most world record titles . That belongs to Ashrita Furman, who is from New York. He has set more than 600 official Guinness Records and currently holds 226 records.

#385 The longest wedding veil was longer than 63.5 football fields.

#386 The world record for the most drinking straws stuffed into one's mouth is 459.

HISTORY AND DATES

For some people, history is a boring topic, an uninteresting subject we were taught in school and for which we had to remember useless dates and numbers. What is *Industrialism*? When did it start? How long did the *Second World War* last? Who was fighting against whom...and so on. But it's important to keep an open mind.

History is more than simply looking backward; it's also critically engaging with the present and learning about the future. To study the past, we don't have to become a professional historian, and anyone who's a curious citizen can do it. When you start engaging with the study of history, you will see that it is much more than learning about kings and governments. It contains the understanding of societies across the world and how they lived over centuries. This teaches us to think analytically, creatively, and to interpret all kinds of information.

But history is even more than that; it is about families, nations, the community. In short, history is about life. These days, huge contemporary challenges of inequality, migration, and climate change require a long-term perspective. By looking at the past and studying the timeless qualities of human behavior, we can make more informed choices about the future.

#387 *Mariner 4* was the very first spacecraft to visit Mars; it was launched in 1964.

#388 The construction of the *Eiffel Tower* started in 1887. Originally, it was planned to be erected in Barcelona, but the project was rejected because citizens thought it was an eyesore.

#389 In 1916, when a producer wanted to enhance the eyes of an actress in a movie, false eyelashes were invented. The lashes were made of human hair.

#390 During WWII, the very first bomb dropped on Berlin killed the only elephant in the *Berlin Zoo*.

#391 One of the first representations of dreadlocks dates from 1500 BC in the *Minoan Civilization,* one of the earliest civilizations in Europe, who lived in what is now known as Greece.

#392 Women have used makeup since before Cleopatra's time. In those days, they used berries and other fruits to give their faces some color.

#393 Back in 1971, *Creeper,* the first computer virus ever, was created.

#394 The earliest mention of the unicorn dates back as far as 2700 BC in Asia. The mythical creature was described as a being of great power and wisdom.

#395 *"Banca Monte Dei Paschi di Siena"* is the world's oldest surviving bank. It was founded in 1472 and is currently Italy's 3rd largest bank.

#396 *Aleksandr A. Serebrov,* a Russian cosmonaut, took his *Game Boy* to space in 1993. It is said to have orbited earth 3,000 times. Later, this legendary *Game Boy* was auctioned for $1,220.

#397 In 1986, because of a bet with the co-pilot, a soviet Aeroflot pilot tried to land the aircraft blindly with all the windows curtained. The plane crashed and killed 70 of the 94 passengers on board.

#398 The *"Pinky Promise"* initially indicated that the person who breaks the promise must cut off their pinky finger.

#399 In 1942, a 12-year-old boy lied about his age and joined the *Navy*. But he was thrown out after his mom found out.

#400 Liège (Belgium) attempted to use 37 cats for delivering mail in the 1870s. Unfortunately, most the cats took up to a day to deliver the post. Therefore, the service was short-lived.

#401 The biggest snowflake in the world was found in 1887. It was 15 inches (38.1 cm) wide and 8 inches (20.3 cm) thick.

#402 The first living creature sent into space was a dog called *Laika* (1957).

#403 It took the radio 38 years to reach a market audience of 50 million people. The television was a little faster with 13 years. But the iPod only took 3 years to get a market audience of 50 million.

#404 A woman was arrested on a beach in Boston (1907) for wearing a one-piece swimsuit.

#405 When *Einstein* died in 1955, his brain went missing and was lost for 23 years. It was stolen and hidden by the doctor who worked on his autopsy.

#406 The oldest present flag of a sovereign state is the Danish flag. It was adopted in 1370 or earlier. The second oldest is the Netherlands' flag, which has existed since 1572.

#407 *Tutankhamun's* parents were cousins. And the pharaoh himself married his half-sister.

#408 The very first roller coaster was used to transport coal down a hill. Some people found out that it could reach speeds up to 50 miles (80 km) per hour. After that, tourists asked to ride on it for a few cents.

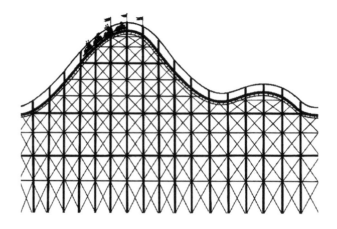

#409 The first designer logo ever was the famous *Lacoste* crocodile. The symbol was created in 1933.

#410 *Coca-Cola* was first served in 1886. At that time, only nine colas were served a day and 3,285 a year. Today, on average, 19,400 Coke products are consumed every second.

#411 *Mickey Mouse* was the first-ever cartoon character to talk. His first words, "Hot dogs!" appeared in the 1929 episode, *The Karnival Kid*.

#412 The first jet aircraft was invented in Germany. The development started in 1936, but the first takeoff occurred in 1939.

#413 The United Kingdom prints its laws on vellum, which is made from calf or goatskin (since 1497). They continue to do so in order to uphold the tradition (which is heavily discussed).

#414 The first photograph ever shot, the 1826 photo called *The View from the Window at Le Gras*, took 8 hours to expose.

#415 In South Korea, on *Valentine's Day*, only women give gifts, not men.

#416 Plumbers in America call the day after Thanksgiving *"Brown Friday"* because it is their busiest day of the year.

#417 The 29th of May is officially *"Put a Pillow on Your Fridge Day."*

#418 *Doug Engelbart* created the first computer mouse, which was made from wood, in 1964.

#419 In Italy, an entire courthouse was built to prosecute the Mafia. The trial lasted from 1986-1992, and 474 members were charged. To this day, it was the biggest trial in the world.

#420 The 17th of January is known as *"Ditch New Year's Resolution Day."*

#421 In the British Museum, a snail was glued to a specimen card (mid-1800s). After four years fixed there, scientists realized it was still alive.

#422 On the 1st of April in 2005, *NASA* pulled an April Fool's prank telling the world they had found water on Mars.

#423 The odds of being born on the 29th of February are 1 in 1,461.

#424 The 3rd of December is known as *"Roof Over Your Head Day"* – a day to be grateful for what we have in life!

#425 The Vatican played music, which was forbidden to be copied. It was a secret for almost 150 years until the 14-year-old *Mozart* heard it and transcribed it from memory.

#426 In 1992, a cargo ship traveling from Hong Kong to the United States accidentally lost a shipping crate in the Pacific Ocean. Nearly 30,000 rubber ducks were lost at sea. Today, they are still being discovered at various beaches.

#427 Soviet Russia built automated lighthouses powered by small nuclear reactors because they needed light on their uninhabited Northern Coast.

#428 In world history, the longest unbroken alliance is between England and Portugal. It has lasted since 1386, and it still stands today.

· 13 ·

LANGUAGE AND LITERATURE

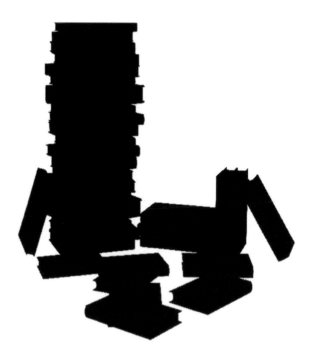

Because of the many different countries and cultures existing in the world, there are also various means of communication and languages. Today, roughly 6,500 languages are spoken on the earth. Sadly, some of them are endangered due to the dynamic communities whose lives are shaped by the rapidly changing world. *Busuu,* for example, is only spoken by 8 people in Cameroon.

Other languages, however, are spoken by huge populations around the globe and are often popular choices among new language learners. Looking at the numbers of total speakers, *English* takes first place with 1,132 million people. However, if we only consider native persons, *Mandarin Chinese* is unbeatable, with its 918 million native speakers.

You've probably heard how challenging it is to learn Mandarin; you need to know around 2,500 (from a total of 50,000) characters to understand 98% of written Chinese. What makes it even harder is that Mandarin is a tonal language, which means that based on the way we pronounce a word, it changes its meaning. One upside is that it doesn't contain tenses, verb conjugations and gender-specific nouns.

English is totally different because of all the tenses and rules that apply. Don't worry, now we're going to look at language and literature from a different perspective, starting with this teaser right now: The word *"goodbye"* was originally an abbreviation of "God be with ye."

#429 *Arctic* and *Antarctic* derive their names to the meanings of "Bears" and "Opposite the Bears."

#430 Malta's official language is *Maltese*. The bulk of the population also speaks English.

#431 The word *"peacock"* doesn't apply to both the male and female birds. Only the males are called *peacocks*, while the females are called *peahens*. The collective name for both of them is *peafowl*.

#432 *Kiss* means "pee" in Swedish.

#433 The letter *Z* is the least frequent letter in written English. It's less common in British English than in American English due to spelling differences, such as "recognize" vs. "recognise."

#434 We all recognize the complexity of the Chinese language. But did you know that the most challenging modern Chinese character requires 23 total strokes to write? This is quán and means "cheek bones."

#435 The word "Android" stands for
a robot with a human appearance.

#436 The band *Led Zeppelin* originally wanted to be
called *"Lead Zeppelin,"* but they felt the "thick
Americans" would pronounce the word wrong.

#437 *NASA* is the short version of "National
Aeronautics and Space Administration."

#438 The anxiety of peanut butter
sticking to the roof of your mouth
is called *Arachibutyrophobia.*

#439 *Puma, cougar,* and *mountain lion* are
names for the same animal. The scientific
name is "puma." However, they are more
commonly referred to as "cougars."

#440 Stimulating the salivary glands underneath
your tongue and then spitting a concentrated
jet of pure saliva is called *Gleeking.*

#441 *"Zugzwang"* comes from German and
means when you have to make a choice,
and every option is a bad one.

#442 The origin of the word *"white"*
is from the Indo-European word
"kweit," meaning *to shine.*

#443   *"Musa sapientum"* is the Latin name for
banana, which translates to "the fruit of the
wise men."

#444   Many Greek athletes
trained naked for
the Olympic games.
That's why the
word *"Gymnastics"*
linguistically means
"to train naked." It
is derived from two
Ancient Greek words: *gumnasía* (athletic
training, exercise) and *gumnós* (naked).

#445   The word *"oxymoron"* is itself an oxymoron
(two contradictory words appearing
together), due to the fact that it derives
from Ancient Greek where "oxy" means
sharp, and "moros" means stupid.

#446   *"Darth Vader"* is derived from Old Dutch,
literally meaning "Dark Father."

#447   *"Schnapsidee"* (English, schnapps-idea) is
the German word for a ridiculous idea that
only sounds good when you're drunk.

#448   *"Astronaut"* is a compound word derived
from two Ancient Greek words: "Astro"
meaning *star* and "naut" meaning *sailor*.
So astronaut means *Starsailor*.

#449 In Indonesian, there is a word, *"Jayus."* It means "a joke told so poorly and so unfunny that one cannot help but laugh."

#450 The Greeks didn't understand foreign languages and thought it sounded like the other people were saying "bar bar bar" all the time. That's why the word *"barbarian"* originally referred to people who don't speak Greek.

#451 *Twelve* is the largest number in the English language that has just one syllable.

#452 *Bi-weekly* can mean two different things: twice a week, or once every two weeks.

#453 J.K. Rowling got rejected by 12 publishers before the original *Harry Potter* pitch finally was accepted.

#454 The word "almost" is one of the longest in the English language to have all its letters in alphabetical order.

#455 *Eminem's* mother filed an $11 million defamation lawsuit against him (because of his lyrics about her). From the $25,000 she settled for, $23,354.25 of that went to her lawyer.

#456 One *Horsepower* is about 746 Watts. That term was coined in the late 18th century, and one horse can have approximately 15 horsepower.

#457 The terms *"Mr."* and *"Mrs."* originated from using the words *master* and *mistress*.

#458 The English language is not native to the British Isles. Outside invaders displaced Britain's native Celtic speakers and introduced a new West Germanic language.

#459 *Webster's Dictionary* accidentally had a word that didn't exist in it for five years – it appeared as *"dord."*

#460 The only letter which doesn't appear on the periodic table is *"J."*

#461 Even though Irish is the official language in Ireland, Polish is more widely spoken.

#462 *Samsung* means "three stars" in Korean. The founder chose this because he wanted the company to be powerful and everlasting like stars in the sky.

#463 *"IKEA"* is an acronym standing for *Ingvar Kamprad* (the founder's name) *Elmtaryd* (the farm where he grew up) *Agunnaryd* (his hometown).

#464 In English, to leave a party without telling anyone is called a *"French Exit."* In French, it's called a *"partir à l'anglaise,"* which means to leave like the English.

#465 It is believed that *"sixth sick sheik's sixth sheep's sick"* is the toughest tongue twister in the English language.

#466 *"Scraunched"* is the longest one-syllable word in the English language. Two other long, one-syllable words are "screeched" and "strengths," but they only have 9 letters.

#467 *"Dreamt"* is the only English word that ends in the letters "mt."

#468 With 9,690,000 characters *"A la recherche du temps perdu"* (written by Marcel Proust) is the longest book in the world. It tells the author's experiences growing up.

#469 In the English language, there are only 4 words that end in "dous": *tremendous*, *horrendous*, *stupendous*, and *hazardous*.

#470 *"Stewardesses"* is the longest word that you only need to use your left hand to type.

#471 *Orange* rhymes with only one word in the dictionary: "Sporadenge." It means a structure in which spores are produced.

· 14 ·

OTHER AMUSEMENTS

The world and everything that comes with it is infinite. You will never know everything, and there's always more to learn and experience. Even if you think you're an expert about a specific topic, you should stay humble and be open to new knowledge and ideas. Keep learning, exploring and researching. That's what makes our life exciting and entertaining.

This book could be huge with the unlimited amount of facts around the world, but who wants to carry around such a big thing? However, your brain is different. It can soak up as much information as you wish without getting any larger or heavier. After a while, it may be difficult to take in any more knowledge because the brain gets exhausted. But the point is that we should be grateful for this gift of a computer-like organ and make good use of it. I encourage you to start (or continue) exploring and not to lose the joy of discovery.

That being said, here come some random facts about other fun stuff.

#472 *Shakira* was rejected from the school choir because her vibrato was too strong. The music teacher in second grade told her she sounded like a goat.

#473 The second-largest purchaser of explosives in the United States is *Disney World* (due to fireworks, etc.). The first being the *US Department of Defense*.

#474 In 2007, a full 1,000-gallon (3,785 liters) inflatable swimming pool was stolen from someone's back yard. A single drop of water was not found!

#475 In Japanese legend, it is said that if you fold 1,000 origami cranes, you will be granted a wish by the gods.

#476 The police in Belfast (Northern Ireland) became creative and used music from an ice-cream van to calm down angry teen rioters.

#477 One in every four cranes on the earth is in Dubai.

#478 It took the Triangle nearly 100 years to become a popular orchestral instrument.

#479 When kissing somebody, around 70% of people tilt their heads to the right rather than the left.

#480 Around 125,000 people get a speeding ticket in the US, every day.

#481 *Albert Einstein* was married to his first cousin, *Elsa Einstein*.

#482 *King Kong* (1933) was the first movie ever to have a sequel.

#483 While filming the Harry Potter movies, *Daniel Radcliffe* broke over 80 wands because he used them as drumsticks!

#484 In Iceland, there's a dating app available that stops you from hooking up with your cousin.

#485 The inflatable pig attached to the power station broke free when *Pink Floyd* designed the "Animals" album cover, causing *Heathrow Airport* to cancel multiple flights.

#486 *Ed Sheeran* (born in 1991) has a ketchup bottle tattooed on his arm.

 #487 The word "friends" is said in every single episode of the Friends series.

#488 A customer of a pizzeria "tipped" the waitress $3,000,000 because she helped him choose the numbers for a winning lottery ticket in 1984. The waitress got half of his $6,000,000 prize money.

#489 In Japan, there is a company with schools teaching you how to be funny. The first one opened in 1982. Each year, about 1,000 students take these courses.

#490 *SpongeBob's* voice actor and the voice actor of *Karen* (Plankton's computer wife) have been married since 1995.

#491 In 2005, a 22-year-old man whose name was *Ronald MacDonald* robbed a *Wendy's*.

#492 Some lipsticks contain fish scales.

#493 Eight of the ten biggest statues
in the world are Buddhas.

#494 Bubble wrap was originally invented as
wallpaper. The creators tried to make a
wallpaper out of plastic with a paper backing,
but it came out with plastic
backing.

#495 The Pokémon *Hitmonlee* and
Hitmonchan are based on
Bruce Lee and Jackie Chan.

#496 Elizabeth II, the *Queen
of England,* has two
birthdays. The day of
her actual birth (21st of
April) and one to celebrate with a proper
parade when it's not as cold as in April.

#497 The American President *Lyndon B. Johnson*
(1908 - 1973) owned a water-surfing car.

#498 *Justin Bieber's* very first tweet was at
8:27 pm on the 11th of May, 2009.

#499 Fredric Baur, who was the founder of *Pringles*, requested to be buried in a *Pringles* can in the 1980s. His children honored the request.

#500 Originally, movie trailers were shown after the movie, which is why they were called "trailers."

#501 The oldest "your mom" joke was discovered on a 3,500-year-old Babylonian tablet.

#502 According to director David Fincher, there is a Starbucks coffee cup in every scene of *Fight Club*.

#503 Seven percent of American adults really believe that chocolate milk comes from brown cows. That's more than 16 million American people.

#504 In 2017, more people died from injuries and accidents caused by taking a selfie than by shark attacks.

#505 The 100 folds in a chef's hat represent 100 ways to cook an egg.

#506 The first living passengers in a hot air balloon were a sheep, a duck and a rooster.

#507 If you recycle one glass jar, it saves enough energy to watch television for 3 hours.

Before we head to the very last chapter of this book (where you can test your knowledge), I would appreciate if you left a review by clicking right <u>here</u> or scanning the code below. It only takes 60 seconds to write some short sentences, and this would really help me out. I'm sending greetings to you in advance.

Amazon.com/review/create-review?&asin=B096TTR9VX

Quiz

Now it's time to test yourself. How many facts can you remember? How much knowledge have you accumulated? The following quiz shouldn't be perceived as some sort of test or learning control. But you can use it as a refresher of your brain, and it allows you to realize how much you've learned.

Maybe this information will be of great use for you when you're taking part in a TV show, and one of these questions is the key to win. Or maybe you can play this quiz with your friends, and you will be able to look smart next to them.

Every question is on the left-hand side and the associated answer at the right. I advise you to cover the right-hand side with a sheet of paper or something like that. Then uncover the solutions line after line while you're trying to answer the quiz correctly. Or you could invite someone to ask you the questions for even more fun. This way, after you've heard the solution, you might have something interesting to discuss.

These are just suggestions. I don't want to tell you how to handle this book because you should use it how you want and in the way it's most enjoyable for you and everyone else. Have fun!

1) What happens when you keep a goldfish in the dark?

It becomes pale.

2) Which animal can see UV light?

Reindeer.

3) On what special place of the body do bumblebees have hair?

On their eyes.

4) What is the world's largest marsupial?

Kangaroos. They keep growing until they die.

5) What is the world's smallest mammal?

The *Bumblebee Bat*. It weighs about the same as a US dime.

6) Where is the viaduct the *Hogwarts Express* from the Harry Potter movies drove over located?

In Scotland.

7) What percent of the London Underground actually is under the ground?

45%.

8) Where is a town called *Santa Claus*?

In Indiana.

9) How long is the spectacular *Great Wall of China*?

It is 21,196 km (13,170 mi) long.

10) What country does not have a railway system?

Iceland.

11) What was the first soft drink ever consumed in space?

Coca-Cola.

12) On which planet is the tallest mountain in our solar system, *Olympus Mons*?

On Mars.

13) Who suggested the name for Pluto?

An 11-year-old girl.

14) What was the first food eaten by humans in space?

Applesauce.

15) Flying with a spacecraft, how long would a trip to Pluto take?

9-12 years.

16) On a genetic level, is the fungus more closely related to animals or plants?

To animals.

17) What did Robert Chesebrough eat a spoonful of every single day?

Vaseline, which he invented.

18) What is a natural way to deal with sunburn?

Applying non-fat yogurt to a sunburnt area.

19) How many football fields of peas are grown in the UK in a single year?

70,000.

20) In Japan, what animal was tested for doing *Domino's* pizza delivery?

The reindeer.

21) What is the second most popular sport in the world?

Cricket.

22) What are Olympic gold medals made of?

Silver.

23) What were golf balls originally made of?

Cow or horsehide and stuffed with feathers, most often from goose.

24) How many muscles are you using with every step you take?

200.

25) How long did the longest cricket test match last, which was held between England and South Africa?

Over 12 days. It only finished because the English team would have missed their boat home.

26) How many trees are cut down daily to supply the world's toilet paper?

27,000.

27) What was the most expensive domain name that was sold for an astonishing $872.3 million?

Cars.com

28) Why can deep snow appear blue?

Because the extra layers of snow create a filter for light.

29) What happens if you heat a magnet?

It will lose its magnetism.

30) What are the odds that in a room with 23 people, 2 of them will have the same birthday?

There's a 50% chance.

31) What is the "sleepiest country" in the world?

New Zealand. The average Kiwi sleeps nearly 7h 45min per day.

32) How many bones are in a human foot?

26.

33) What will happen if a human being tries to walk in a straight line while having a blindfold on?

The person will gradually walk in a circle.

34) How long does it take a red blood cell to make a complete circuit through your body?

Only about 1 minute.

35) How many times does a human eye move per second?

About 50 times.

36) Are you allowed to use the *Netflix* account of your roommate or friend?

No, sharing a *Netflix* password is a federal crime.

37) How many different haircuts are Northern Korean women allowed to have?

They have to choose from 15 haircuts.

38) What is illegal to wear while committing a violent crime in New Jersey?

A bulletproof vest.

39) In *Halden prison,* guards are encouraged to interact, play sports, and eat with the inmates. Where is it located?

In Norway.

40) Where is it illegal to die?

In *Svalbard,* a remote Norwegian island, and *Sellia* (Italy).

41) When was the first paper money made?

It was made in China, over 1,000 years ago.

42) What is the world's most expensive object ever built?

It's the *International Space Station* (US $150 billion).

43) Who holds the record for appearing on the most currencies?

Queen Elizabeth II (born in 1926), who appears on the currencies of over 35 countries.

44) What is the oldest currency in the world which is still in use?

The British Pound (1,200 years old).

45) How many ways exist to make change for a dollar?

293.

46) Does the color *red* make bulls angry?

No, they are color-blind.

47) How do frogs drink water?

Through their skin.

48) For how long do elephants stay pregnant?

For 22 months.

49) What is the only fish that can blink with both eyes?

The shark.

50) Which animals struggle walking backward because of the shape of their legs?

Kangaroos and emus.

51) For which company was the largest advertising poster, measuring 28,922.10 m² (311,314 ft²), produced?

For *Arby's* (American fast-food chain).

52) How long is the longest nose of a living person?

It measures 8.8 cm (3.46 in) from the bridge to the tip.

53) What is the longest time someone voluntarily held his breath?

24 min 3.45 s.

54) *Eminem* holds the world record for the most words in a hit single. What's the name of the song and how many words does it contain?

The song is called "Rap God" and is packed with 1,560 words.

55) What was the length of the longest wedding veil?

It was longer than 63.5 football fields.

56) Where was the *Eiffel Tower* originally planned to be erected?

In Barcelona.

57) When was *Creeper,* the first computer virus ever, created?

In 1971.

58) Where does the name *"Pinky Promise"* come from?

It initially indicated that the person who breaks the promise must cut off their pinky finger.

59) What was the size of the biggest snowflake, found in 1887?

It was 15 inches (38.1 cm) wide and 8 inches (20.3 cm) thick.

60) How were Tutankhamun's parents related?

They were cousins.

61) What is the least frequent letter in written English?

The letter Z.

62) What does *Kiss* mean in Swedish?

It means "pee."

63) What does *NASA* stand for?

It is the short version of "National Aeronautics and Space Administration."

64) Where do the terms *"Mr."* and *"Mrs."* originate?

From the words *master* and *mistress*.

65) Which word from the dictionary rhymes with *orange*?

Sporange, a structure in which spores are produced.

66) What is the second-largest purchaser of explosives in the United States (after the US Department of Defense)?

It is *Disney World*.

67) How many people get
a speeding ticket in
the US per day?

Around 125,000.

68) In which country is a
dating app available that
stops you from hooking
up with your cousin?

In Iceland.

69) Why are movie trailers
called "trailers?"

Because they
were originally
shown after
the movie.

70) How many American adults
believe that chocolate milk
comes from brown cows?

7%, that's
more than 16
million people.

Do you want more fun facts? Then join our _Fantastic Fun Facts Community_ on Facebook. It's an awesome group where we share and discuss amazing facts, daily. I hope to see you there soon :)

Conclusion

Finally, after 507 outrageous facts, we end our adventurous journey. I hope you enjoyed reading this exciting information and can make good use of it (more or less). Now you don't have to worry anymore about finding yourself in an awkward moment of silence. You can simply whip out an absurd fact and start making the conversation more fun. Hopefully, you keep your curiosity for learning more, and maybe we'll meet again in the future. As you made it this far, I wish you only the best.

By the way, let me know what the best chapter was and maybe I will create a book on your favorites. You can do this by clicking the link below:

https://starkingbooks.activehosted.com/f/7

PS: If you haven't already, please <u>review</u> this book. Thank you so much, and enjoy your life!

Amazon.com/review/create-review?&asin=B096TTR9VX

Resources

40 Interesting Money Facts. (2018, 14th June). Retrieved 23rd June, 2020, from https://www.seriousfacts.com/money-facts/

50 Random Facts that you Won't Believe are True. (2020, 23rd April). Retrieved 25th June, 2020, from https://kidsactivitiesblog.com/76701/50-random-facts/

Animals - mom.me. (n.d.). Retrieved 22nd June, 2020, from https://animals.mom.me/

Arora, M. (2020, 14th January). 50 Spellbinding Science Facts for Kids. Retrieved 18th June, 2020, from https://parenting.firstcry.com/articles/50-spellbinding-science-facts-for-kids/

Bellis, Mary. (2020, 11th February). A Brief History of Sports. Retrieved from https://www.thoughtco.com/history-of-sports-1992447

Bennett, J. (2019, 31st December). The Top Ten Scientific Discoveries of the Decade. Retrieved 19th June, 2020, from https://www.smithsonianmag.com/science-nature/top-ten-scientific-discoveries-decade-180973873/

Cabello, M. A. P. J. S. &. (2019, 6th October). What Japan can teach us about cleanliness. Retrieved 17th June, 2020, from http://www.bbc.com/travel/story/20191006-what-japan-can-teach-us-about-cleanliness

Consumption Of Sugar-Sweetened Drinks Tied To 180,000 Deaths Each Year. (2015, 2nd July). Retrieved 17th June, 2020, from https://www.nwphysicians.com/consumption-of-sugar-sweetened-drinks-tied-to-180000-deaths-each-year/

Daniel, A. (2020, 17th April). 100 Fascinating Facts You'll Want to Share with Everyone You Know. Retrieved 18th June, 2020, from https://bestlifeonline.com/crazy-random-facts/

Eaton, V. (2018, 14th May). 9 Oldest Sodas in the World. Retrieved 22nd June, 2020, from https://www.oldest.org/food/sodas/

ENIAC, World's First Computer. (n.d.). Retrieved 25th June, 2020, from http://www.pimall.com/nais/pivintage/enic.html

Fun Facts for Kids about Sports. (2018, 8th August). Retrieved 21st June, 2020, from https://easy-scienceforkids.com/sports-science-fair-projects-facts-for-kids-video/

Guetebier, A. (2020, 4th June). 81 Amazing Facts Every Kid Should Know. Retrieved 18th June, 2020, from https://redtri.com/quirky-facts-and-trivia-for-kids/slide/1

Home. (n.d.). Retrieved 19th June, 2020, from https://www.guinnessworldrecords.com/

How Many Times Does Your Heart Beat in a Lifetime? (2020, 27th February). Retrieved 16th June, 2020, from https://www.wonderopolis.org/wonder/how-many-times-does-your-heart-beat-in-a-lifetime

Maddison -, A. (2019, 7th September). Busuu Blog - language learning tips, inspiration and news. Retrieved 23rd June, 2020, from https://blog.busuu.com/

News: Breaking News, National news, Latest Bollywood News, Sports News, Business News and Political News | Times of India. (n.d.). Retrieved 19th June, 2020, from https://timesofindia.india-times.com/

NIEHS Office of Communications and Public Liaison. (n.d.). Kids Environment Kids Health - National Institute of Environmental Health Sciences. Retrieved 20th June, 2020, from https://kids. niehs.nih.gov/games/riddles/jokes/

Nova. (1996, 26th October). The History of Money. Retrieved 18th June, 2020, from https://www. pbs.org/wgbh/nova/article/history-money/

Picard, C. (2019, 27th December). 35 Coolest Random Pieces of Trivia That Will Impress Your Friends. Retrieved 21st June, 2020, from https:// www.goodhousekeeping.com/life/g25692093/ random-trivia/?slide=2

Say "Prunes," Not "Cheese": The History of Smiling in Photographs. (2012, 4th November). Retrieved 20th June, 2020, from https://petapixel. com/2012/11/04/say-prunes-not-cheese-the-history-of-smiling-in-photographs/

Science Kids. (n.d.). Retrieved 15th June, 2020, from https://www.sciencekids.co.nz/sciencefacts/

Siegel, E. (2019, 20th December). How Many Planets In The Universe? - Starts With A Bang! Retrieved 24th June, 2020, from https://medium.com/ starts-with-a-bang/how-many-planets-in-the-universe-9153a05bd0d5

Space.com Staff. (2012, 1st March). How Long Do Footprints Last on the Moon? Retrieved 20th June, 2020, from https://www.space.com/14740-foot-prints-moon.html

The 25 Most Unbelievable Sports FACTS! - SportsPickle. (2018, 17th May). Retrieved 19th June, 2020, from https://medium.com/sportspickle/the-25-most-unbelievable-sports-facts-41d3d6521679

The Editors of Encyclopaedia Britannica. (2020, 18th May). Pangea | Definition, Map, History, & Facts.

Retrieved 18th June, 2020, from https://www.britannica.com/place/Pangea

The Fact Site | Fun & Interesting Facts. (2020, 23rd March). Retrieved 21st June, 2020, from https://www.thefactsite.com/

Tobin, Declan. (2020). Fun Facts For Kids About Sports. Easy Science for Kids. Retrieved from https://easyscienceforkids.com/sports-science-fair-projects-facts-for-kids-video/

Walsh, G. (2020, 8th June). 37 fantastic facts that will blow your kids' minds. Retrieved 19th June, 2020, from https://www.goodtoknow.co.uk/family/facts-for-kids-5446

Wikipedia contributors. (2020, 15th June). China at the Olympics. Retrieved 18th June, 2020, from https://en.wikipedia.org/wiki/China_at_the_Olympics

Printed in Great Britain
by Amazon